The Water Cycle

by Robin Nelson

first step nonfiction

Lerner Publications Company · Minneapolis

All water on the earth is
part of the water **cycle.**

The sun warms the water
in the oceans.

Heat changes water into a gas called water **vapor.**

Water vapor rises into the sky.

The water vapor cools and
turns into tiny **droplets.**

These droplets make **clouds.**

The water droplets stick together inside the clouds.

The droplets get heavier and
fall to the earth as rain.

The rain runs into a **brook.**

The brook flows into
a stream.

The stream flows over
a waterfall.

The waterfall flows into a river.

The river flows into
an ocean.

The water is warmed by
the sun again.

The water will turn
into vapor.

The water cycle starts again.

The Water Cycle

A cycle is when things happen over and over again in the same order. The water cycle is one example of a cycle. Water in the ocean turns to vapor. The vapor forms a cloud. The cloud is filled with water droplets. The droplets fall as rain. The rain flows into the ocean. The water turns to vapor again. The cycle repeats over and over again. Can you think of any other cycles?

Water Cycle Facts

 Raindrops are not shaped like tear drops. Raindrops are shaped like hamburger buns.

 Water that has turned into water vapor spends about ten days floating in the air.

 The water we use today is the same water that was here when the dinosaurs lived.

 Acid rain is rain mixed with pollutants from cars, volcanoes, and big factories.

Acid rain can kill plants, hurt animals, and pollute our drinking water.

 The process of water turning into water vapor is called evaporation.

 The process of water vapor becoming a liquid again is called condensation.

Glossary

 brook – a small path of water; a brook is smaller than a stream

 clouds – large groups of water droplets floating in the air

 cycle – things that happen over and over again in the same order

 droplets – tiny drops

 vapor – small bits of water in the air

Index

The photographs in this book are reproduced through the courtesy of: PhotoDisc, front cover; Minneapolis Public Library, pp. 2, 12; © Rob & Ann Simpson/ Photo Agora, p. 3; © David Kreider/Photo Agora, pp. 4, 16, 22 (bottom); © Mark Keller/SuperStock p. 5; PhotoDisc, pp. 6, 22 (second from bottom); © Jeff Greenberg/Photo Agora, pp. 7, 22 (second from top); © Gary Bass/Photo Agora, p. 8; © Robert Maust/Photo Agora, pp. 9, 17, 22 (middle); © Stephen Graham Photography, pp. 10, 11, 14, 15, 22 (top); © Colleen Sexton/Independent Picture Service, p. 13.

Illustration on page 18 by Tim Seeley.

Lerner Publications Company
A division of Lerner Publishing Group
241 First Avenue North
Minneapolis, MN 55401 USA

Website address: www.lernerbooks.com

Library of Congress Cataloging-in-Publication Data

Nelson, Robin, 1971–
      The water cycle / by Robin Nelson.
         p.   cm. — (First step nonfiction)
      Summary: Summarizes how Earth's water changes to vapor and rises into the sky where it turns into rain, and introduces related concepts such as the shape of raindrops and the presence of pollutants in rainfall.
      ISBN-13: 978–0–8225–4596–5 (lib. bdg. : alk. paper)
      ISBN-10: 0–8225–4596–9 (lib. bdg. : alk. paper)
      1. Hydrologic cycle—Juvenile literature. [1. Hydrologic cycle. 2. Rain and rainfall.]
I. Title. II. Series.
GB848 .N46 2003
551.48—dc21   2002007190

Manufactured in the United States of America
4 5 6 7 8 9 – DP – 11 10 09 08 07 06